To Our Young Readers:

We have now written many stories about remarkable animals. But we had been looking for a story about pandas—one of our favorites. It is said that the giant panda is the cutest animal in the world. Their large heads, black eyes, and furry black-and-white coats make them almost seem like giant stuffed animals. So when we saw pictures in the newspaper of scientists at the Wolong Conservancy in China dressed up like giant stuffed pandas we wanted to know more.

This is the story of an experiment to release one little giant panda, Tao Tao, who was living in captivity, back into the wild. Along with help from his mother, Cao Cao, and many scientists and panda experts, Tao Tao was being prepared to be the first panda returned to the wild. It is very important since only 1,600 pandas remain in the wild while just 300 live in conservancies. If Tao Tao's return to the wild is successful he will hopefully find a mate. The panda is an endangered species. But people will go to great lengths to ensure their survival—even dressing up like giant stuffed pandas. Let us hope the experiment is a success!

With hope for all,

Craig, Juliana, and Isabella Hatkoff

Photographs:
Cover: © Associated Press; Back cover: © Associated Press;
Pages 19 (top), 24 (top), 29: © Wang xiwei cd - Imaginechina
All other photos: © Associated Press

ISBN 978-0-545-43410-2

Text copyright © 2012 by Turtle Pond Publications LLC

10 9 8 7 6 5 4 3 2 1   12 13 14 15 16 17/0

Printed in the U.S.A.   40
First printing, September 2012

Panda Patrol:

Caring for a Cub

Told by

JULIANA, ISABELLA, *and* CRAIG HATKOFF

SCHOLASTIC INC.

Giant pandas once roamed free across China, but in recent years their habitat has become much smaller. The number of pandas has become smaller, too.

There has been a lot of growth in China, which means more people and more buildings. There is less space for the giant panda.

In 1963, the Wolong National Nature Reserve opened high in the mountains of China. On a reserve, no one can cut down trees to build big highways. No one can hunt pandas. The Wolong Reserve is a safe place for pandas. But they were still in trouble. They were endangered, which means only a small number still lived in the wild. The scientists at Wolong wanted to do more.

Other people wanted to do more, too. World Wildlife Fund, a group that protects wildlife, worked to create other reserves and make sure there were forests where wild pandas could thrive.

Then, in 1980, the scientists at Wolong started the Wolong Giant Panda Breeding Center. The breeding center is similar to a zoo. It has indoor and outdoor spaces for the pandas. It also has a nursery for baby pandas.

It isn't easy to take care of the babies. Sometimes a mother panda is not able to care for her cub.

When the cubs are born, they don't look like pandas at all. They are pink! And they are tiny—not much bigger than a hot dog!

The scientists take good care of the cubs. They take exact notes on everything. The scientists wear special blue lab coats.

Soon, there were many healthy, young pandas at Wolong! But the scientists were still worried. The number of pandas living in the wild was still very low.

The scientists agreed on a goal: They would release cubs born at Wolong into the wild. But would a panda born in captivity know how to live in its natural habitat?

The scientists decided to start with just one cub, named Tao Tao. Tao Tao and his mother, Cao Cao, lived in a special area on the reserve. Here, his mother could take care of him. Here, she could teach him how to live in the wild.

The scientists wanted to check on Tao Tao as he was growing. But they didn't want the cub to see people. Panda cubs do not see people in the wild. So the scientists took off their blue lab coats and put on giant panda suits!

When Tao Tao needed to go to the center for a checkup, the scientists

carried him in a tub. This way, the cub
did not see people.

Tao Tao didn't know he was special. He didn't know the scientists had big plans for him. He was like any other giant panda cub. He liked playing with his mother. He liked to tumble and roll. He liked to investigate his world.

The scientists knew Tao Tao was special. They made sure he was growing well. They checked his teeth. They weighed him. They measured him. But sometimes it was hard to hold Tao Tao with panda mittens on, so the scientists used their bare hands.

Tao Tao was adventurous. Like other pandas, he learned to climb trees when he was about six months old. His mom helped him. Climbing is a good skill. It can keep a panda safe.

The cub really liked to climb. Once when it was time for his checkup, Tao Tao scampered up a tree. He made the scientists wait over four hours in their hot panda suits!

The scientists watched Tao Tao closely to see if he could handle life in the wild. By the time he was six months old, he proved that he could climb trees, look for his own food, and be aware of dangers in the forest.

Next, the scientists took Tao Tao to a training area higher in the mountains. The ground was rockier. It would be harder to find food. It was another test to see if he would be ready to live on his own. Luckily, he still had Cao Cao to help him.

After he turns two, the scientists at Wolong will decide if Tao Tao is ready to be released into the wild. Until then,